A Personal Apocalypse

'The Poetic Ramblings of a Troubled Man'

By Jack W Gregory

This book is dedicated to my family, friends, Church and the people that I am blessed to have chosen to share my life with.

£1 from this book goes to:

Hope Community Church, Wymondham (Registered Charity Number: 1126428)

Hope into Action - Helping Churches House the Homeless (Registered Charity number 1137686)

Acknowledgements

I would like to thank all those whom have been involved in this Book.

My partner Joanna for sticking by me through thick and thin.

My daughter Regan for always being my shining light,

Mr Jamie Boyle for having faith, and publishing my work in his books.

Mr Mark James Hiblen for the amazing artwork in this book and for your friendship.

Mr Jim Motram for Permission to use the photo of me and his kindness and friendship through the past couple of years.

Grantley and Floss Watkins for believing in me and showing me the love of God through their ministry, and their teachings and vision through Hope Community Church, Wymondham.

Mr Phil Rowe and Earl Ling for their encouragement over the years and helping me strive for the best.

To Annmarie my editor for your advice and friendship.

Mr Nathan Gregory for the advice, and foreword.

My good friend Ria Landon, not only for the foreword and kind words but for your friendship and trust over many years.

Mr Lee Wortley, for the friendship and kind words in his Afterword.

Joanna Hogg (Director of The Souvenir), for giving me a shot when very few would.

Tom Burke (Actor), for your advice and friendship on set.

Leo Gregory (Actor), for your sound advice, support and friendship.

About the author ....

Long Story Short …

Jack (William) Gregory Is an Actor, Writer, Director, Poet, Photographer, Musician, Producer and Loving Father based in Wymondham, Norfolk, UK. He was born in Glasgow in 1977 and Lovingly Raised by his adoptive parents in Normanton, West Yorkshire.

During his brief 40 years walking the roads of this world He was an accomplished Magician, he Trained briefly as an actor in youth with Local and National Theatre groups.

He trained in creative writing at the Yorkshire Arts Circus under Ian Clayton (albeit briefly). He was a performance poet under the mentor ship and guidance of Karl Dallas (again albeit briefly) winning several poetry awards.

Jack had lived a troubled life for a long time, he not only fought addiction, he fought to escape from crime and violence for many years.

After a Long spell of illness Jack has yet again begun to rebuild his life. His first ever published work comes in the form of Four commissioned poems about Legendary Heavyweight Boxer and Hard-man Paul Sykes, for Jamie Boyle's Best Selling books Sykes: Unfinished agony and Further Agony from War Cry Press.

Incidentally Jack Knew and occasionally worked alongside Paul as a Debt Collector in his younger days.

Jack is now under the care and guidance of Hope Community Church, Wymondham. He is also training under The School of Supernatural Life Program.

Foreword by Maria Landon

International Best Selling Author of "Daddy's Little Earner" and "Escaping Daddy"

I am honoured to be asked to write this foreword for Jack and couldn't be more proud to see his work come into print for there are few people I have met who deserve this more than him.

Jacks poetry will take you by surprise with its raw, disturbing, and uncomfortable subject matter. Sometimes only a few words are needed to take you down those dark alleys where you find the most tortured and tormented souls. Jack takes us to see people we pretend don't exist, people that supposedly don't affect us and no stone is left upturned as our curiosity leads us to the most marginalized and vulnerable people in our society. The homeless, the addict, the criminal, the alcoholic and those living with mental health problems are all there, Jack cares about them all enough, not only to give them a voice through his words but by drawing us in further as we see for example through the pain etched across the woman's' face in his photography.

Jack has a natural affinity with his characters, he strips the label from them and makes them human again and his characters trust him. He is their trustworthy counselor and they know he will not let them down because through his work Jack has given these people the gift of hope. All the time Jack speaks up for them, how can we ignore them?

Brilliant work Jack. Keep it up.

Foreword by Nathan Gregory

Author of "Chromasome Quest"

Writer's motivations are endless. Italo Calvino said that he wrote "to give vent to my feelings and because I like it". George Orwell claimed the drive to write originated with "a Mystery" that the writer was trying to uncover. Maya Angelou said "There is no greater agony than bearing an untold story inside you".

Writing can open a direct connection to our inner self, to understanding who we are.

I have known Jack Gregory for more than four years now. Despite the commonality of surnames, we are not related, but it was that coincidence of surname that led to our connection via my own genealogical studies. We have each since followed our own path towards Authorship and exchanged many notes along the way. His journey of growth and development, coping with addiction, mental and physical illness during the process is worthy of a best seller/

Heinlein said "A poet who reads his verse in public may have other nasty habits", back handed praise for those brave enough to commit their words to paper.

A Personal Apocalypse is both Poetry and Autobiography, a personal journey from the depths of the human condition to recovery and strength. Both Heinlein and Angelou would be pleased.

A letter to Mum and Dad

You took me in and for most, if not all of my adult life, I have treated you so badly. As a younger man you bailed me out of so much trouble, so much debt yet I continued to take advantage. I realize that over the past few years my communication has been poor to say the least.

Over the years I have caused you so much hurt and pain and have taken you for granted. In all my years I have kept all of my pain and used it to fuel my bad behavior, in all of my selfishness I used excuses as to why none of this was my fault, I tried to shift the blame to other people, including you.

The way my life has taken me, the trouble I found myself in has all been my own fault, my responsibility, yet I feel that you have taken on some of that blame yourselves and that is unfair and unjust.

My reasons for keeping away, for having poor contact are due to one thing only, that is my own selfishness. For many years I have blamed myself for treating you so very badly.

As an adult my life choices have been down to me, the decisions I have made were so very poor, yet I would change very little, for the choices I have made, whether good or bad have made me into the person I am today.

I cannot change the way I have treated you, I cannot take back the wrongs I have done to you or even hope to make up for the hurt and anguish you have suffered at my hand, through my life. However, from the bottom of my heart, I humbly ask for your forgiveness. so very sorry for everything I have done to hurt you, to upset and embarrass you.

My life is empty without in it. I do love you, with all of heart and soul, even though I don't show it.

Your Son … William

Introduction

Our Lives are a constant network of winding roads and walkways, street lights and pathways.

The lives we live, the choices we make are roads well traveled. Some take us straight to our destination, some fragment, divert, re root and take us the long way round and some take us in the complete wrong direction. We spend our time searching for the faster route, the easier way, yet if we are not careful the constant wrong route will inevitably lead to ruin.

All so many times in my life I have taken the seemingly easy route, shortcut upon shortcut and ended up lost and alone, helpless and scared trying desperately to find my way.

Each detour and every wrong turn is another story, a different outcome and I have inevitably ended up on many an unwanted adventure, further away from my desired destination, yet miraculously these roads have always led me home, wherever it may be.

So If home is where the heart is, then I find myself divided. For me Home is where my family is yet without a loving father at the helm, guiding me, walking with me so i never have to walk alone then alas I fear I may not be here today.

It was not always like this, my life at times has being a living hell, trapped in constant fear and self loathing, a prisoner inside my own mind. Who would have thought a relationship with the higher power I choose to call God would be my making, after all God is just a made up magic man in the sky is he not ?, and if not how would he ever love a man like me ?.

Many a time I have found myself living an 8x6 life looking out of the window and all I could see, all my blinkered vision would allow was for me to see road.

This book is probably the most challenging thing I have ever written or will ever write. For some, myself included the past is often painful, yet I endeavor to go deeper than I have ever gone to attempt to tell a fuller story. Some of the subject matter in this book tackles many demons from my past, some even my own mother does not know, yet I find myself drawn to showing the full picture of the man that is Jack W Gregory and the events that have shaped me, that have molded me, that have broken me, time and time again . I originally started writing this book several years ago. A Personal Apocalypse is the assimilation of most of the poetry I have written through my life.

Reading and writing has not always been easy for me, I was educated (if you can call it that) in the Mid Yorkshire special school system between the mid 80's to the early 90s. This was a time when Dyslexia was not really seen as a problem, many children such as myself who struggled at school were just seen as either naughty and lazy or just plain stupid, so many of us were lost in the system.

I always had knowledge very good general knowledge and could be pretty smart when I wanted be, I always had a gift of being able to retain and recite knowledge, it was just I was not able to get it down on paper or read it very well, however being knowledgeable in a system where many of my school friends came from broken homes and violent backgrounds and with learning difficulties often greater than my own it opened me up to the world of bullying, not just verbal but often physical and the results were often frequent trips to the hospital.

Went Vale special school was an institution that often rewarded bad behavior and poor performance with outwards bounds activities, I guess they believed that if they could not train the mind they may as well train the body and focus on fitness rather than mental ability, So by the time I left School Education I could still barely read or write, yet I could climb, abseil, teach canoeing and make my way through most of the cave systems in the country.

The only actual qualifications I left school with were a certificate in changing a fuse in a plug, a certificate in riding a 50cc moped and a certificate for answering a private telephone.

I will explain later in the book how and why I began writing poetry, I will however end with this;

Poetry and writing have been my saving grace, a constant crutch to fall back on when my mind has been full of the constant confusion of a thousand thoughts attacking my often fragile mind.

They are my way of venting, of finding release, However they have also been a factor in many a Breakdown, the cause of many a rant and drug fuelled rage, yet like estranged lovers I have constantly sought solace in the arms of my precious writing, tucked up at the breast of the beauty that we call Poetry. My whole adult life I have fought addiction, suicide, violence and the dreaded rabid mutt that is the black dog of mental illness and somehow I still survive.

Over the past 3 years I have been rebuilding my life after breakdown upon breakdown, I have fought addiction, homelessness, loss, PTSD, brain injury, Tuberculosis, Double Pneumonia, trauma and suicidal thoughts, yet by the grace of God I survive another day.

I'm not even really sure what category this book may fall into.

It isn't a full memoir, nor is it an Autobiography. I think the best way that I could describe it would be to say it is a look through the Windows of certain points of my life. A brief look into the mind of a man who not only seen and felt his fair share of pain, he has also caused it

Enjoy the mind of a broken man.

Jack

This is me …

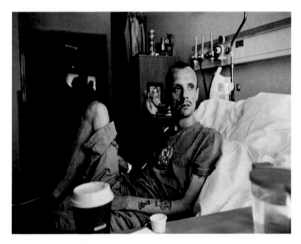

J.A Motram 2015 (used with permission)

This is me before I died

A life lived in Symbiosis, entwined with drugs, violence and lies

This is me, mind Broken body frail

The life I lived was no fairy-tale

This is me

after a life of crime, addiction, lies and living on borrowed time

This is me with illness at unease

crippled with fear, pain and disease

This is me

Wasting away

Knowing time is fading, I am Passing away

This is me before I died

Unknowingly I would be given another chance at life

This isn't me

the old me is dead

I'm not that frail man, bound to his bed

Because this is me

not weak, I am strong

I am love beyond belief

live a life in which I belong

I strive, I fight

I'm Not him any more

Living life well away from deaths door

I have family, I have friends

I have passion and love

I have a life blessed by God

From the heavens above

"We stared into the face of death, and death blinked first. You'd think it would make us feel invincible. It didn't". Rick Yancey - The Fifth

Asleep

Asleep, Asleep … Wrapped in a blanket of darkness

and I find myself falling slowly into my own personal apocalypse

Fighting and punching the walls of sanity

Not knowing who I am, where I am

or where will I go from here

Awake, Awake …My is soul trapped

wrapped in grief and unable to weep for the fear of living to see the end of the word

and Death may take me again at any given moment, yet I welcome her

With arms wide open

for my life has been nothing but a constant storm, causing devastation for all those who had the misfortune to be around me

yet this is only the beginning of the end of the world

For I am cursed and I shall be forced to watch our beloved earth come to a violent end

Because It was I who caused it

Awake, Awake … I shall be the last to see it

to watch it take its final, fading dying breath as the embers and ashes slowly fade away

I shall be there, The murderer mourning, trapped in his personal prison built with bars of guilt and shame. Locked away in an eternal limbo as the event is played on repeat again and again and again

For eternity, a punishment deserved

Asleep, Asleep

The celestial father has now disowned me , for the angels did not come

God himself has succumbed to the fact that the earth shall die by my hand and my hand alone and the devil laughs loudly, standing in the corner his playground

And still the sky is falling and complete chaos reigns on the outside

even a Dystopian world would be better than this

the Four Horsemen are well and truly on their way

This Dying world once divided by war and famine now united in hatred of me

Yet I am unable to shed a single tear in fear that I may be seen to be weak in my final moments

and my final breath will be welcomed by so many

God no longer cares and even the Angels dare not stand on this unholy ground

I know all this, yet I still cannot shed a tear in regret

for I am broken through and through

Not even God will save me now!

Illustration M.J Hiblen 2017 – (c) Jack W Gregory

I

The Apocalypse begins

I have deliberated for so long about where to start this book, at the very beginning?, at the end?, or somewhere in the middle?, this is a posing question even at the time of writing so as these are The Poetic Ramblings of a Trouble Man then I shall just attempt to let my mind flow and my fingers do the work.

March 15th 2015

As I awoke from my medically induced state my eyes struggled to adjust to the artificial light of the white walled ventilation room I found myself incarcerated in. Dry crusty mucus caused by the oxygen hose blocked my nose, so I could only breathe through my open mouth, and that was with extreme concentration.

My eyes struggled to adjust to the bright medical lights. There I was in a whitewashed room with walls so bright they reflected what little light came through the window into my face. My only view through the window was a brick wall. Dazed, confused and struggling to breathe I pulled the drip pipe from my cannula and attempted to make my escape.

How had I gotten here?, where was I? And what the hell had they done to me?

I moved my legs slowly around to the side of the bed, I felt so weak, yet I was obviously being held prisoner in some kind of medical research facility, I was being tested on, trapped in a total nightmare. As soon as my feet hit the ground and I let go of the side of the bed I hit the floor face first.

What kind of hell was this?

Had I woken up in a movie?, a zombie infested scene reminiscent of 28 days later or The Walking Dead ?. I had no strength to pull myself up; all I could do was slowly slide towards the door to make my daring escape.

In front of me was a hardwood door with a small widow and I could not even muster up the strength to look through it, yet to my left a heavy door that was slightly ajar, I had found my means of escape, now all I needed to do was muster up the strength to claw, to crawl and make my way to freedom.

Somehow I managed to push the door open a little more and grabbing th door frame I managed to pull myself in and onto the bobbled bathroom floor. It took every ounce of my strength to drag myself up on to my knees so I could pull myself up onto the shower chair to sit down to regain my failing, rattling breath and the pain in my chest was intense.

I looked up to the mirror above the clinical white porcelain sink, who was this man looking back at me ?. Emaciated and white with a yellow tint to his skin, his eyes bulging from the tight skin covered skull that resembled something quite alien.

My lips Cracked, dry and blistered, swollen beyond recognition. My chest blistered, inflamed where the undercover policemen had laid an acid laden sheet to torture me, to extract information, and it burned so badly, the pain was maddening and soul destroying, but I deserved nothing less.

I heard the door with the window pushed open violently and commotion ensued, my heart had begun beating fast, if felt like it was going to break through my already frail and Belson like chest. It was fight or flight and I had strength to do neither, perhaps it was just time to die. I fell limply to the floor and rolled in front of the door in a feeble attempt to barricade myself in, my attempts were futile.

The door burst open with ease and rolled me over with a force. I looked up and stifled a scream as the masked men, reminiscent of characters from some sort of contagion movie leaned over glaring at me, I could feel the hate from their eyes burning into my soul, I could not understand the muffled voices as I pathetically tried to put up a feeble fight, I felt a painful jab into my right buttock and all went black.

I don't know how long I was asleep, unaware of my surroundings. The room felt different, the air was heavier and I must have slept a long while as my clean shaven face was now awry with matted facial hair. Mouth dry, I could barely swallow yet I dared not drink the water as I feared it was tainted, poisoned with my own blood, a ploy to keep me sick whilst the drugs kept me partially sedated.

I trusted no one, especially the ones I knew. Facebook had gone down days ago as it flooded with the news of betrayal of this earth, i had poisoned it with my dirty breath. I always thought weapons of mass destruction would end this earth, turned out it was a northern monkey poisoned it with the contagion of tuberculosis and God knows what else, I was a test subject, a living incubator for any and all nefarious and insidious diseases that could bring about the end of the world.

Trapped in a state of limbo, the fine line between sleeplessness and exhaustion. Sirens intermittently sound letting me know 1 more million people had died, another reason to torture me. Outside the sun was failing and the world was falling. Outside the very building I was hostage in was home to rotting corpses , remnants of friends, family and the unlucky , and It was I that caused this, If only I could cry, If only I could show how sorry I really was then maybe, just maybe the would stop the torture and let me die, Instead of this hell.

The room next door was awry and cram packed with the people I once knew, I once loved and who once loved me, now united in hate and the common goal of watching me suffer.

The ones who died were replaced by robots, by clones or just clever disguises, they would intermittently visit to try to fool me, deceive my very soul and tell me everything was going to be fine, yet in secret they would hold kangaroo court and agreed to let me die if everyone would agree and the only one who wanted me to live, to just make me better and live out my days destined to be the last human was my niece Hayley, she kept me alive out of love not hate.

Every torture technique, mental and physical I took because I knew I deserved it, however there were some that broke me. Bear this I believed that most of my family had died of either shock or disease. My Girlfriend had been brainwashed, and fed lies through an earpiece every time she visited, forced to try to get me to take poison, to get me to eat poisoned food tainted with my own deadly blood, I knew their game so I would not eat and eventually I would die of starvation on my own terms. My daughter had died days before and I was being forced to video call with her whilst they used her like a puppet to try to fool me.

I just wanted to die, why would they not let me die ?.

Grantley, the lead pastor from my church had come in to read me my last rights, but he knew that the end of day were here and I was destined for hellfire because the angels dare not come because the demons were ravenous.

My friend Paul Julian would visit because his faith in God was so strong he just wanted me to repent, but this was not Paul, this was a robot designed to fool me.

Two weeks later …

I don't know when things began to get better, to get easier and clearer. The fear, self loathing, paranoia began to subside. The hallucinations, the voices and the hate were gone. The fog on my brain was clearing and after years of dipping in and out of religion, pretending to be a Christian to excuse my behavior I finally accepted Jesus Christ into my Live and from Death I was reborn .

My life has gotten better over the past 2 years or so, not that it has been easy, I have dealt with some real personal trauma and tragedy, but with the help of my church, with the help of my friends and my little family, with Joanna my partner and our respective children I have begun to grow in faith, in strength and love.

I am now in a position where I can write about it, share my life, my experience, my strength, my weakness and hope to try to help other people recover from Mental Illness and find a purpose in life.

So comes this book, these ramblings of a troubled man in an attempt to shed so light on the messed up world I created for myself and the events that eventually led to a very personal apocalypse.

Childhood Dreams

(Dedicated to Mum and Dad)

Childhood dreams and fantasies

echo through my memories

I remember the calmest seas, sailing toward an island of seal

Remember oh father remember

It seems like only yesterday

It seems like only yesterday

when in the garden we would play

with action man and Lego bricks

whip and top, pick-up sticks

remember oh sister remember

it seems like only yesterday

it seems like only yesterday

when I fell and broke my arm

and when I awoke from unconsciousness in the armchair

there you were ironing, telling me I'm going to be OK

keeping me calm

remember oh mother remember

it seems like only yesterday

II

Some memories fade or are limited, however there are some that are so vivid, so life changing that they stay with you for the rest of your natural life. The events that affect us, that mold us and shape us deviate in detail at times, dates can be forgotten and details can combine to create unintended untruths or inaccuracy.

DONT GET ME WRONG, I WAS LOVED, BEYOND DOUBT.

I was never mistreated by my loving and gentle parents. My failings as a son have always been my own, my fault, my responsibility, and for that I take full ownership, although for many years I wrongly blamed them for my shortcomings. Its so easy to blame others for our failings, when in fact we should own our behavior.

Anyway I digress.

I don't remember having many friends at all and my relationship with the kids on my street was somewhat rocky at times. I remember playing with the Lindsey the girl next door and her friend next door to her also called Lindsey. The other lad on the street Tim whom I played with from time to time who lived 3 doors away would often tease me with his friends for playing with girls, I guess I always preferred the company of the opposite sex.

The only other lads in the area were a little older so tended only to hang around when they had nothing better to do.

I never really went without anything, I always got what I needed and all to often whatever I wanted, you could say that I was more than a little spoilt. My sister already in her mid to late teens would often be out with her friends so that just left me and my parents would often take me into Wakefield for dinner and a Toy, in retrospect I think maybe my want for the newest toys and clothes were to compensate my my feelings of loneliness and isolation.

My mother was known as a caring woman, well know throughout the town. She worked with Social Services as a Carer for many of the old people around, I believe her job now a days would be classed as a domiciliary or something along those lines. I love my mum, I was always a mummy's boy.

Most Saturdays would be spent with my father, being a Civil Engineer for British Rail had its advantages, mainly the free train travel to anywhere in the UK. We would often get up at 5 or 6 am on a Saturday armed only with a pack up and my dads light brown leather holdall. I remember telling him once that we were doing about Scotland at school so on the Saturday he took me to Edinburgh just to get me a Scottish pound note and a postcard to take into school, these would become the days that I miss so much. My Dad the traveler, my Dad the hero. A man so loved and cared for by the community in which he still lives in today. He would do all sorts of jobs such as painting and decorating for the older residents of the area in which we lived.

Dad in the garden chopping wood, old flat capped Fred wandering aimlessly, whistling his merry tune whilst he walked his little Jack Russel. "Ey up old cock" he would chirp at me over the wall and give me a wink before nattering to my dad for what seemed like ages, then without a signal or a clue he would wonder away and whistle, look back and tip his flat cap.

One of My first and strongest memories teeter around the age of 8 around 1985. In my teenage years and my adulthood I had convinced myself that this was my 8th birthday, I don't know whether it is out of fear I have not asked my parents but this event unintentionally led to the beginning of my downfall. This is how it plays out for me, it is not untruth but as the event plays in my mind.

One thing I do know, one truth that will never fail, that will never fade or falter.

This is how I remember it, this is when my life began to darken and I began a slow, painful journey to many different rock bottoms.

A day of presents, a day of love, a day of cake and treats, of fizzy pop and not to mention a Brand new Wig-Wam in the back garden. Playing with my friends until the afternoon became evening.

One content happy little boy sat upon his mothers knee cuddled in watching The Grumbleweeds on ITV. My mother with nothing but love in her eyes, yet her smile crooked and an air of sadness lingered around her. The conversation is a little mixed up in my head, some details are lost but it plays out in my head like this.

She gazed lovingly into my baby blue eyes and whispered those 3 words that make any little mummy's boy smile.

"I Love you"

And I smiled, I may have blushed

a blonde little mummy's boy and heaven was found upon her knee.

My father sat on his sofa reading the tabloids occasionally gazing over

his glasses offering reassurance.

"You know that don't you, you know I Love you, that we love you"

an unfamiliar tremble in her soft, northern voice.

"yes mam, love you too"

Tears held back rested in her eyes as she ran her soft fingers genteelly down my little face.

"Nothing can ever change that, nothing that can ever be said or ever be done will ever change that fact, we are your mum and dad, always remember that ".

She took a breath and did her best to hold back the flood of emotion, yet a stray tear rolled down her cheek.

"We love you so much but I have to tell you that we are not your real parents,

We are your mum and dad but you have another mum,

a real mum who I'm sure loves you very much but can not look after you, so we have you,

We chose you and adopted you and became your Mum and Dad"

How could they not be my parents?, how could my sister not be my sister ?, I could not retain any information whatsoever, all I wanted to do was cry.

Confusion set in, tearful, hurt I didn't know what was real anymore I began to cry and my fear of rejection, my fear of loss, that fear that would become the fuel for my behavior, the excuse for the way I lived my life.

THIS WAS THE DAY THAT THE LIGHTS WENT OUT FOR ME AND THERE WAS NOTHING THAT ANYONE COULD HAVE DONE TO CHANGE THAT FACT !.I know that this must have been the hardest thing to do in their life, to love someone else's child and to be a parent, to love them to the end of the earth and have to tell their child they are adopted must be soul destroying.

I don't blame my parents for anything, I love them for they are mine but my behavior towards them, my excuses, my deeds and my lies have hurt them so much, In my own stubbornness, in my own fear and my own guilt I did not communicate with them for several years. I would find excuses, reasons not to but one thing resounds in my mind.

I HAVE HURT THEM SO MUCH, YET THEY STILL LOVE ME BEYOND A SHADOW OF A DOUBT. THE PAIN I HAVE CAUSED THEM IS INXCUSABLE AND ALL I CAN EVER HOPE IS THAT ONE DAY THEY WILL FORGIVE ME.

My problem was that I did not want to be me, I felt hurt, confused and unwanted even though my mum and dad would go above and beyond what most parents would do just to try and please me.

I would tell the most awful lies at school and quickly became known as a billy liar. I would steal, I would cause trouble. Tantrum upon tantrum I would play up to be the loudest, the Centre of attention. I was bullied because of the way I was, I was bullied because I was different, because of the way I behaved and I was on the road to becoming a monumental nightmare for my family, In fact I was becoming a monumental Knob. As I grew older my lies got bigger, more elaborate, more dramatic. Did I mention I had a flair for the dramatic, I would use this to my advantage a few years down the line, to make money, to make trouble but I cant help but feel I did this the hide from the reality that I just wanted to cry all the time and escape from the prison I called my mind.

Thank You

When you close your eyes

what do you see

do you see the poor man that is me

It's not being poor from the lack of material things that bothers me

it's the fact I am losing my dignity

oh my darling

please don't cry

wipe away the tears from your eyes

I just want to thank you

for loving me

like you do

like I love you

for 20 damn years

I gave them my life

they took it away

piece by piece

oh my darling

please don't cry

wipe away the tears from your eyes

I just want to thank you

for loving me

like you do

like I love you

my muscles are aching

I cannot breathe

black lung blues, I cough up coal

I can't get no relief

oh my darling

please don't cry

wipe away the tears from your eyes

I just want to thank you

for loving me

like you do

like I love you

the angels are here now

to take me home

to take me to a better place, for you, for me

Don't cry my darling

I'm going to be with our family

so before I set out

on my journey anew

there is one last thing I would like to say to you

I just want to thank you

for loving me

like you do

like I love you

III

Growing up in a small Yorkshire town during the 1980's and 90's certainly leaves an impression. There were several collieries within such a short distance. Normanton, once an affluent market town began to decay. During a recent visit home I saw for myself the effects of the pit closures had on local businesses.

It has not changed in the 2oish years since I left. Many of the thriving businesses, Pubs and shops now faded over time.

Anyway I deviate from my original point.

Normanton was failing way before I left, in fact I still have memories in my early childhood of buildings in disrepair and an estate of council properties in tower blocks were already aging and failing.

My Grandparents Luther and Anne Gregory lived on Dalefield Rd, now my memory fails me so I am not sure whether it was 101 or 111, not that it matters anyway.

I absolutely idolized my Granddad. He seemed so old, so wise but he was an aging man yet he seemed so strong. I have vivid memories of him carrying 2 bags of coal mounted upon his strong shoulders through the house to the bunker in the back garden.

I remember fondly after my grandmother died he moved in to sheltered accommodation just around the corner. He had this old wooden cabinet with a glass front. I don't know what else he kept in it but he would always cut the front and back from empty cereal boxes that he kept for me to draw on. Incidentally he also had a sock draw that he would keep 50ps in an old black sock and dish them out to me and my sister for pocket money.

In the early 1980s, Normanton was full of role models most boys aspired to be, an affluent market town with ties to the local coal industry and on a direct rail route between Wakefield and Leeds.

When Thatcher run Britain hit and the proverbial hit the fan, collieries closed, miners went on strike and the unions stepped in, the town began to fail as many of the miners came from the town.

I can't really say that it affected my family too much as my father worked on the railways but the fallback on the town was devastating for many families, the town still keeps going, but its hard to go back an see my home for so many years frozen in time.

I digress

Many year later, towards the end of my grandfathers life he was living in a nursing home on Heath Common and even though I only lived a short walk away I found it hard to visit, he was very frail and Alzheimer had well and truly taken a hold, the once strong, charming and funny man now reduced to nothing but confusion. When I did visit him he would talk about the war, the industry and the local mines and the men that shaped his life.

This poem was inspired partly by him and some of the families that I knew but also in part inspired by a singer songwriter Martyn Joseph and his song Please sir, Martyn is an absolute hero of mine and incidentally I would get to perform this as a song for him after one of his shows in Norwich about 10 years ago, It also serves as a memory to my friends father who died due to Pneumoniconiosis (Black Lung) after many years exposure to the coal dust.

The Schoolboy and The Dragon

Illustration Lorne Mosley 2017

A wolf in sheep's clothing is suffocating my already fading soul

I am left shattered, crying in the rain

nursing my broken hopes, dreams and goals

AND IT IS KILLING ME

Killing me slowly

Killing me quick

Draining my fading life force

making me

SICK

Sick from the anger

sick from the pain

A waterfall of emotions

Cascades through my neural pathways

flooding my brain

AND I AM DROWNING

It is drowning me slowly

Drowning me quick

draining my life force

making me

SICK

The sickness forms from deep within the dark and vast chasms within my
poisoned mind, body and soul

AND NOW THE PAIN BEGINS

My cotton wool mind

my fading, dying, suffocating soul

My dreams how they are diminishing, fading

strangling my hopes, my goals

AND IT IS KILLING ME

Killing me slowly

Killing me quick

Draining my fading life force

making me

SICK

AND ALL BECAUSE THE SCHOOLBOY CHASED THE DRAGON,
AND THE DRAGON BURNED, SCORCHED HIS EVER FADING
SOUL

Killing me slowly

Killing me quick

Draining my fading life force

making me

SICK

IV

My school days are some of the most poignant yet upsetting days of my life. I always found it such a painful place. My earliest memories of my school days take place at Normanton Town Middle School or Normanton Grammar as it was more commonly known.

It was an old Victorian building and somewhat intimidating. I was never really very good, I didn't understand the lessons so I would play up so I didst have to write, I couldn't really read or write well at all. I could sort of copy but if it was off my own steam I failed miserably. Mr Shackleton the headmaster was a nice enough fellow, he taught a lot of me as did my 3rd year teacher Mr Cook, the others just thought I was a bit of a handful I guess.

Mr Shackleton would let me work with my imagination at break times and let me make up my own mini one man plays that I would perform in the staff-room before the end of the day, I guess it was easier for them to let my mind wander than spending the afternoon looking for me because I hated Physical Education. Inevitably at some point someone would upset me and I would trash the odd classroom. The only things I excelled at in those schools were failure and lies.

I have no idea how I did it but I even managed a year in Freestone High School. The problem in those days (mid to late 80s) were that Dyslexia was not well known, like many my age that stumbled through the school system haphazardly were either seen as thick, as lazy or as both. Don t get me wrong I had a brilliant mind for retaining General knowledge ad useless information, I just couldn't get it down on paper.

So after a year of stumbling I was moved into the special school system and that's where the real trouble began. I was very much a little fish in a pond full of sharks, totally out of my depth and at a loss. I never really had good people skills, that mixed with being very physically weak and having knowledge even though I could not write it down, well it left me an easy target for the bullies.

Went Vale was a school (an I use that term loosely) that rewarded bad behavior with outward bounds activities, so by the time I left there I could abseil, canoe, climb, ride a 50 cc moped but still I could barely read or write my name, In later life I found my way just winging it to get through.

I left school with no formal qualifications whatsoever as there was no exam process, we were taught the basics, hence my early national record of achievement had only certification for things like answering a private telephone, riding a 50cc moped and changing a fuse in a plug.

Towards the end of my education I was bullied almost every day. The last time I was really bulled it resulted in a fight with Trevor Scott behind the bike shed. Not that you can call it a fight, he hit me, I hit the floor and the rest of the fourth year proceeded to kick me in the head for what felt like an eternity. The police were involved , he was expelled and I was never bullied again. The one thing that incident taught me was that actually I could take more punishment than I thought, all I needed to do was learn to fight.

The school itself was situated at the end of a private road next to Carleton High School, a main road at the top, a housing estate to the side then nothing but fields.

Towards the end of my time there I had gotten to know some of the local criminal element, I was told that I needed to stay low key. I hated sports but did like running cross country after I applied myself. Towards the end I could run the 1500 meters in 7 minutes flat, so on a lunch time I could run a delivery of porn videos, pirate VHS films, cassette albums and cannabis and still be back for tapioca pudding.

That is when I really fell into the darkness and decided that I would be anyone else but me, I had lost myself and really fell into the world of violence and deceit.

Illustration M. J Hiblen 2017 (c) Jack W Gregory

"Self-Harm - the world will come at you with knives anyway. you do not need to beat them to it ". Catlin Moran - How to Build a Girl

Skin Deep

She cuts because she hurts

she hurts because she cuts

the compulsion sits and festers, deep within her gut

AND IT HURTS

the boy she likes doesn't notice her

her mum, she always drinks

the kids at school they tease her

Call her fat and say she stinks

AND IT HURTS

she cuts because she feels she has to

she cuts because it hurts

she cuts just to feel the pain

for she feels it's all she is worth

AND IT HURTS

at night, whilst she is dozing

he creeps into her room

he tells her no one will believe her lies

so she cuts just to see the wound

AND IT HURTS

she cuts just to feel it

she cuts to see it bleed

she cuts because it hurts

she cuts to find relief

AND IT HURTS

No one ever sees it

she hides it under clothes

She conceils the scars upon her arms and legs

so no one ever knows

AND IT HURTS

V

As I said School was always a difficult time for me, whatever school it was. I only managed a year in High School before I was moved to a Special School in Pontefract. I really struggled to cope in such a large environment, plus dyslexia wasn't regarded as much as a problem as it is nowadays. I'm not sure if I was seen as lazy, unmotivated or just plain thick, I am inclined to think it was a mixture of all 3.

I never had many friends and the ones I did have were not the sort of friends to boost a man's confidence, I was often the butt of jokes and cruelty all in the name of humor.

Claire was different, she actually genuinely cared about me, I guess because she felt different herself. Often a loner as was I, so we quickly began to forge a friendship through the isolation of others. She always wore long sleeves so I didn't notice the scars at first, it was only when she was caught off guard coming out of the girls changing rooms and forgot to roll her sleeves down. She was so embarrassed, her cheeks now flush red and she hung her head. I just smiled, put my hand on her shoulder and told her that it was alright, I didn't understand what it was or how to deal with it and just told her she was beautiful anyway. She smiled an awkward smile and just carried on walking.

I was moved to Went Vale the following year so we quickly lost touch, I was devastated, I thought I would never see my only friend ever again.

Several years later after having a little trouble in Pontefract I let my friend look after my bedsit and went to stay with my musician mate Wayne who lived with a kindly older lady by the name of rose on Smawthorne lane in Castleford. This haven was affectionately known as Rose's Halfway House for Wayward Creatives. Rose had a soft spot for wayward young lads and just wanted to mother them and use creativity to help them become better more productive members of society.

Thursday night was 10p a Pint night in Legends Nightclub and we had a fiver each and we planned to drink all the watered down Pish we could. I haven't a clue how we got back but I woke up with a screaming hangover, so after loosing the contents of my stomach I headed for the medicine cabinet and found the bottle of paracetamol. As I looked in the mirror all I saw was the shadow of a lad, A Loser, A Disappointment and a Let Down to my family so without thinking, without hesitation I swallowed every single pill in the cabinet and stumbled from the bathroom and straight out of the house, after all I would not want rose to find me like this, I think I got as far as the subway and collapsed.

I awoke swiftly, choking as I felt the pain of a plastic tube being forced down my throat followed by liquid charcoal and gipped as the grit hit my stomach. I began flailing, fighting with all of my strength, attempting to pull the tube from my throat, muffled screams filled the room and as quickly as I awoke I was asleep again courtesy of a sharp painful scratch in my backside and the liquid cosh hit me like a ton of bricks.

Four or five days later I had worked my way around the psych team at Pontefract General Infirmary. I had promised that I wasn't really trying to kill myself, I just had a headache I could not get rid of, I was confused etc. They did not section me at that time but I needed to stay in hospital for a few more days for observations.

I had never needed a fag so much in my whole life but there was no one in the smoking room so I wondered outside dressed in my hospital PJ's with a fashionable Intravenous Drip attached to my arm, I knew there would be someone smoking down there so I could cadge a fag, If not I would raid the ashtray for dimps.

So there I was, smoking a dirty dimp in a world of my own, mind racing at a thousand thoughts a minute as it always did, wondering what would happen next in the horror novel I called my life when my process was interrupted by a silky soft and gentle feminine tone.

"Well, well Mr Gregory, Looking a little rough, do you have a light ? ".

I turned to be greeted by a cheeky friendly grin. Her long black hair tied back in a loose pony tail. He brilliant jade green eyes although dulled and tainted over the years with pain and sorrow still had a slight twinkle. Dirty gray joggers and a dark blue dressing down over a fading white t-shirt.

My heart began to beat to a different tone, one of familiarity, one that I had felt a long time ago. She had barely changed facially, her smile, her eyes were still as hypnotic as the day we met.

We were in a relationship for a little while, however we were both on a destructive path and there was no stopping either of us. She left my flat one morning and never came back, I can only pray that she found some peace in anyway she could.

'

The house that drugs built

This is the house that drugs built

this is the man that lived in the house that drugs built

this is the cell

that now holds the man

that lived in the house that drugs built

this is the stash and the cold hard cash

that was made by the man

who now held in a cell

who lived in the house that drugs built

this is the girl

with a habit formed

who went to the house that drugs build

the same girl

her body worn

because of habit formed

who sold herself in the house that drugs built

she sold herself

to pay for the drugs

because of habit formed

she had to pay the man

the man with the stash and the cold hard cash

who is held in a cell

who lived in the house that drugs built

This is the needle

filled with smack

that was sold to the girl

with the body worn and the habit formed

from taking the drugs

sold by the man

the man with the stash and the cold hard cash

who is held in a cell

who lived in the house that drugs built

this is the bed

where the girl was spread

with needle in arm

where she lay dead

overdosed

her body was worn

because of habit formed

from taking the drugs

sold by the man

the man with the stash and the cold hard cash

who is held in a cell

who lived in the house that drugs built

this is the coffin

where the girl laid to rest

the girl with the body worn

from the habit formed

from taking the drugs

sold by the man

the man with the stash and the cold hard cash

who is held in a cell

who lived in the house that drugs built

this is john

he works for the police

he had to tell the girl's father

who was stricken with grief

little girl is dead at only 19

the girl in the coffin

with the body worn

from the habit formed

who sold herself

to pay for the drugs

from the man with the stash and the cold hard cash

who is held in a cell

who lived in the house that drugs built

VI

Dedicated to the memory of Felix Dennis - 27/05/47 - 22/06/14

I have a little confession. This poem was heavily influenced by the work of poet Felix Dennis, especially his poem, The House That Crack Built.

Incidentally, I was honored to meet Felix at The Playhouse in Norwich where he was on tour shortly before his death. Felix was a very funny and humble human being who had been a hero of mine for many years. I was first introduced to his work when I was given an audio CD of his work from his book, A Glass half full. I immediately fell in love with his work.

Anyway I digress.

I met Sam whilst I was working as a Fixer and Closer for a small firm based running mostly Long Cons in the Leeds and Wakefield area. On a couple of jobs Sam was brought in and used as a Honey Trap to extort high ranking middle aged officials in the area.

She was a young single mother who lived on a council estate in Gipton near Leeds. She was a very beautiful young woman who by the time she was 18 had 2 children, the oldest being 4 and the youngest barely 18 months old. On the outside she appeared to be a confident, Intelligent young lady, she was funny and friendly but on the inside she was screaming and addicted to Heroin, trapped and despairingly struggling to escape.

From the age of 11 she had been repeatedly by abused by a female member of her family and struggled to deal with that along with the confusion about her sexuality. At 13 she begun to run away from home, however she would always be found and put back into the home she fought desperately to get away from so she decided to put a plan into place. She would sell her body to raise the money to set herself up a home as soon as she legally could leave home, after all she could save a lot in two and a half years couldn't she ?.

One day whilst "working" she met a guy who promised her the world. He said he would set her up in a home if she needed to get away, she of course agreed, problem was he had her addicted to Heroin is such a short time.

The House That Drugs Built is based loosely on the events that led up to her death. She was found dead with a needle in her arm behind a high rise block of flats near Gipton. Although I had only met her a couple of times I really felt for her, It wasn't too long after that that my own habit began to begin to overtake my life.

Mother's Joy

As I lifted my head

a single tear rolled down my dirty cheek and fell to the floor like a raindrop
to a rose

as i looked into her deep hypnotic eyes, I could feel the love ebb from
every pore of her body

she looked at her son with nothing but love

they were in constant conflict, a battle of hearts

because all he did was tear her heart apart

the black sheep of the family

the naive naive of hearts

(note) The simple fact is that this Poem is based on the relationship between my Mother and I. Over the years I had caused her so much pain, hurt and suffering. She always supported me, she was always concerned about my welfare, I do not or did not blame her for the way my life turned out, It was just y own stubbornness that stopped me communicating with her for many years, I hurt her and am still seeking to make thing better to this day.

"A friend who dies, it's something of you who dies" Gustave Flaubert

Darren

you caught me

when I was falling

you took me into your arms

you held me close

you held me tight

so I would come to no harm

as I lay there screaming

cursing your very name

you just held me patiently

told me you loved me all the same

as I lay there crying

not knowing where I was

delirium set firmly in

believing that I was lost

you held me tight

you pulled me close

then you mopped my brow

over and over you just said

I love you brother

until the screaming stopped

Big Man, Big Heart

Darren Nigel Livesy - 06/10/66 to 16/08/99

VII

I wrote this the Day I learned Darren Died.

Darren N Livsey was my Best Friend in the world. There is nothing I could ever do to repay the gratitude I have for that man. Darren was so much more than a friend. He was my teacher, my mentor and a brother. Darren taught me not only everything he knew about magic, he taught me to begin to read and write. He was the biggest fan of my poetry and took me to every open mic night and poetry Jam he could find. He also introduced me to a hero of mine who would become a friend for a few years afterward, well known writer and poet Karl Dallas who unfortunately died a couple of years ago.

Darren was the one who introduced me to sobriety from drugs for the first time after locking us both in his spare room and sat through cold turkey with me. He took every insult, ever attract and showed me more love than most have ever shown me, I miss him dearly. After I left Pontefract to try to build a new life I lost contact with his family especially his daughters. I now speak to them every now and again through Facebook.

In September 1996 I had moved into a bedsit on the first floor in a block of flats in Pontefract. It was around this time that my life had begun to majorly fall apart. My drinking was out of control for most of the time I lived there, and by then I had already been attending a twelve step program of recovery for nearly 2 years without much avail. Don't get me wrong, I had times of short abstinence from alcohol, enough time to have the odd break of sanity, but drugs came calling and myself indulgent, selfish and excessive personality shone through and I began to show signs of falling apart in a major way.

I met him through a mutual friend we called 'Big Lad', he had that name for a reason, 6ft 7 inches and 20is stone by the time he left school, Darren stood at 6ft 4 inches and 18 stone. It was by chance I found out he lived on the floor above me. We had quite a lot in common so it was no surprise that we hit it off. We had a mutual love for the art of magic and illusion and would practice together, he did however loath my neighbor and had very little respect for the people that I spent my time with, he vowed to keep me as busy as possible. It was not long before we began working together, among the many other things he was a traveling DJ working mainly in clubs. He taught me the art of mixing, the love of working, the glory of friendship and the one thing I had lacked for so long in my life, that thing was respect.

I always had a love for words, for poetry but I could not write it down, we would spend many a night in his flat drinking whiskey (He never saw alcohol as my problem as he always managed to keep me under control) and holding the world to rights, this would usually end up in him asking me to give him a poem, which I always did, He was my biggest fan.

He made me sit down and began teaching me to write well enough to get the poems on paper, I would always get the hump and screw up the paper and throw it away, problem was he kept them, he sent them off to several poetry competitions and I won a few awards, he kept my trophies and I got them back when he died.

Anyway I digress

We would often travel cross country at the weekends and he would watch me in awe as I performed my poetry in rooms with other poets, we even performed magic at several festivals together under the name Urban Magic.

The one thing Darren loved more than magic, more than music , more than anything, he absolutely loved and adored women, they were on many an occasion his kryptonite. He had started seeing a lady from a nearby town as as he quite rightly spent more time with her, I was left to fend for myself and if there is one thing I proved back then was that I was quite inept at doing that, in fact one of the things I was very good at was self destruction and I had pressed that button many a time.

I had not seen my best friend in a month or so, I was well and truly hooked and back on the drugs, I sought solace wrapped in the wings of my beloved Dragon. I did my best to hide my habit, I would smoke up in the shed downstairs after all I did not want my friends to know my dirty little secret. Wrapped up warm on a winters morning I retreated to the shed, Tin foil in one hand, gear in pocket and I chased her till her breath suffocated my sadness and I could taste her kiss until I fell slowly, softly into slumber, then all went black. I have no idea how long I was out or how I ended up in Darren's spare room. I awoke screaming I absolute agony, my stomach was on fire, churning and a vice like grip just under my diaphragm. All I wanted was to kiss her again, I longed, I needed to be with her yet I was lost, apart from my love and unable to get to her, I hadn't even opened my eyes properly yet and I just wanted to die a quick painless death, what kind of hell was this ? .

I would get to her at any cost, however there were three problems that I could see in the haze. Number 1 the door and widows were locked, number 2 their was a 6 ft 4, 20 stone giant reading Viz Magazine at the bottom of my bed and number 3 I was a 6ft 1, 7 and a half stone weakling unable to do anything but scream obscenities at his best friend who quite frankly at that time his worst enemy.

I wrote a poem for his funeral but unfortunately through time it has been lost and forgotten. A few years later I wrote the following poem and although it does not make up for the original it serves as a memory of the great man.

The Junkie

Desolation

Deprivation

Fused together in a junkies haven

Isolation has demolished the junkies heart

and sent his mind worlds apart

Idealistically rehab is what he needs, but his habit is hungry

so his habit he feeds

His soul cries out from deep inside

crying for freedom from the dungeon of lies

His heart is burning, turning, churning

in a cyclone of despair

so he punches the walls and pulls out his hair

he changes his habit

from drugs to booze

after all he's got nothing to loose

then after a while drink becomes his master

now he's back on the road, the road to disaster

then one day

in a fit of desperation

he ran into a railway station

threw himself onto the track

now for junkie there is no turning back

the train came towards him at a tremendous speed

now there is no more habit for junkie to feed

IX

This was probably the first real poem I wrote and one of Darren Livsey's favorites. He made me write it for him sat at his living room table. I remember being disappointed in the way it was written and screwed it up and threw it away. After I left that night Darren retrieved it, typed it up and sent it away to several small poetry competitions along with a few other pieces of my work. To my surprise they received quite a lot of attention and even won a few small local poetry awards.

Throughout my life I have adapted it into several scripts and works. The most recent being a screenplay I began to write in 2008 ish. The poem was not the only thing to make it into the script, I used Cal's story, His life and his death as part of the main plot. By the time I had finished the first draft it had become apparent that the work was at least semi autobiographical. His life and death has probably affected me the most throughout my adult life.

It was the morning after the week before. We had started our bender at around 9 am on the Wednesday morning. We were unusually flush after a series of events had left us with almost a grand each to use frivolously. We had filled up our cupboards with food and drink, topped up the utility meters with nearly a hundred quid and we were still feeling flush.

An early hearty breakfast at 7.30am at the Redbeck Cafe and motel would see us right for the legendary session ahead, this was followed by a couple of lines of our friend 'charlie' and a few good gulps of whiskey from an old battered and beaten hip-flask to warm the cockles on this brisk winters day. Armed with our trusty Day-rover ticket we started out tour of Yorkshire on the trusty old buses. After Leeds, Huddersfield, Barnsley and Doncaster our next stop was Bradford and that is where it all gets a little hazy I'm afraid.

Cal's brother Eric was a Dealer who lived in Tong on the outskirts of Bradford, so armed with a bottle of White Lightening Cider each, A shed load of Fag Papers and several ounces of Tobacco we set out to spend some time with his older sibling. That is where it all went mental.

We were greeted at the door by several large steroid fulled well dressed Asian fellers, they were friendly enough but you could feel the distrust hovering heavily in the hashish infused air, we were greeted by his brother with open arms and the bender had well and truly begun. I'm afraid I remember very little more until the last day.

We were cooked, done, absolutely battered from our adventure. We had slept very little in 5 days and eaten even less. Not that we were particularly hungry but Eric's hospitality extended to a full English Breakfast before we left. The Tremors had started and the forks on the plates made a porcelain melody. The sweats had started and the sickness had begun. Our pockets near enough empty, only enough for a small bottle of lightening and the travel fair home we decide that we wanted to get back to his as quick as possible so a Trip by train it was. Problem was we didn't think it through and got on the wrong train and ended up in Normanton.

My mum and dad lived there but I could not face seeing them in this state. I know that they would have been welcoming but in all honesty I could not bear my mum seeing me in this ungodly state, so In our Infinite wisdom we decided to walk to his mother's house a few miles away, so we staggered along on our journey.

Cal, Like me has always been mentally troubled, He however had the added pressure of years of sexual abuse from his father. On the way we needed to grab some rest and roll a smoke with the tiny amount of baccy and weed we had left. I don't even really remember where we were, all I remember is It was outside a Level Crossing, We sat down to demolish the rest of the cider and blitz the joint.

Cal began to cry. I asked him what was wrong, he just shook his head until he softly spoke as the thunder of a distant drain rumbled In the background.

"What are you talking about ya daft sod" I replied

"Don't matter " he murmured as he flung his arms round me and In a second he was up an off like a shot.

"WHAT YOU DOING?"

I shouted and before I knew it he had vaulted the level crossing and was hit by the train.

It all plays back so slowly, the memory I mean, what could I have done but beat my fists on the asphalt till they bled.

That day will never leave me that memory will never fade, I still carry the pain of that day even whilst I sleep.

Saturday

Once upon a Saturday night

an angry young man went looking for a fight

A fight he got, a fight he found

He ended up in a hole in the ground

X

It was the mid 90's and Marcus was a highly volatile, chaotic and troubled young man.

19 years old, his whole life set before him, cut short in a single moment of anger. By time he reached 14 he had already seen too much for a young mind to bear, hurt personified tenfold from the events he had been forced to witness. a mind so young yet an intelligence that could match and even outweigh some teachers of the day.

Both of his parents were high functioning alcoholics, his sister pregnant at 13 and his own addictions escalating out of control.

Angry at everyone, everything and bitterly aggrieved with the world around him. The week leading to his death had been a destructive one, not only for himself but for all those around him.

I had met Marcus on a government employment training scheme for an extra tenner a week added to your dole money. I can't claim that we were best friends, that would be a lie, in fact we had crashed several time and that usually ended in violence and I would always come off worse. We did however live on the understanding that I didn't bother him, he didn't bother me and after a couple of drinks we were actually quite friendly, any more than that I tended to stay away for health reasons.

I was not there when it happened so I am only going by the information I was given.

He had been on an absolute bender, having started drinking 7 am Monday morning and the result by Saturday night was hell on earth. All of that pent up anger and pain ended up in an altercation outside a local nightclub at 3am, he started a fight with a guy 10 years his senior, a fight that he would never finish. His life ended too soon after a fist was plunged was into his throat, he died almost instantly. The man responsible for the death of Marcus was so stricken with guilt he retreated into addiction, his charges were dropped after a verdict of accidental death was brought back, he was found dead several weeks later of a heroin overdose.

Fight Night

Head thumping … Heart pumping

Fists clenched hard

Punching, biting … Kicking fighting

Throw em to the floor

Hit em hard … Hit em right

Watch em hit the deck

Lock his arms and squeeze your thighs right around his neck

It's tap em out or they pass out

Fight, Fight, Fight!

(note) I had several bare knuckle fights during my life, this poem is inspired by the gut feeling before a fight, as the excitement sickens you, the crowds cheer and it's bring on the pain. It was never really a career choice, more of an adrenaline rush that I was rather fond of. To tell you the truth I made more staying down than I did getting up, so win win really.

Photo credit: Jack W Gregory, 2014

My Dragon and Me

For me my addictions have lasted nearly three decades with both long and short periods of sobriety in between. It would be near on impossible for me to remember what frame of mind I was in when I wrote these so I thought I would share these in a single chapter so hopefully you could see what sort of mind I was living in. If I remember any details I will add them as a point.

You may notice I use the word Dragon to describe my Addiction, This isn't from the phrase *"Chasing the Dragon"* as In Smoking Heroin, It is the Alternative name to My Addictive Behavior.

Enjoy !!!

Fallen Knight

Black Knight

Mounted up on his White horse

Chasing the Dragon to kiss her on her tender lips of despair

She holds him tight and tenderly

his head rests up on her scaly bosom, her tail wrapped around his chest

She cradles him and nurses him

into eternal rest

(note) In memorandum of Nathan who died of a Heroin Overdose aged 19. I found him OD'd in his flat at Baghill.

XI

"We are addicted to our thoughts. We cannot change anything if we cannot change our thinking" Santosh Kalwwar - Quote me everyday

BarFly

Running scared … Running fast

Running down the Railway tracks

Chasing hate … Chasing fear

All he wants is one beer

one more beer to end the pain

To stop himself going

INSANE!!!!!!

For most of my adult life all I have ever done is run. Run away from problems, People, Places and situations. My early life was fight or flight and I have to admit it was flight 90 percent of the time. Too scared to stay, too fearful to run, so I would often find myself frozen in a situation, maybe not physically but defiantly mentally and spiritually.

There are many things that overpower, strongholds that keep us locked in a situation time after time.

The film Groundhog Day focused on a man trapped in a single day, this would have been preferable, bliss compared to reliving ever single second, trapped in a constant sorrow, darkness at every single point in time, i could see no end, all i could wish for was the darkness to transform to nothingness, because then at least I would not feel ever again, oblivion is better than the events it follows, isn't it ?.

Her Kiss (A Pi Poem)

There she stands

Seductively

Her face to mine

I stand shaking in my boots

waiting, wondering when her kiss will take me home

her breath

so warn, begins to spread slowly

deep inside my aching lungs

knees go weak

my mind begins to haze

as her venomous breath courses through my body

intent on going deeper inside my suffocating, fading soul

my body now worn from battles lost

battered, bruised and I am burned on the inside

so I cry

silently within

mind now numb

in a state of quickening

she kisses me again

harder, deeper than the kiss before

I weep

a mixture of pleasure and pain

deeper I sink inside myself

body now limp

not yet asleep

Slumber

Slumber Subsides

As I awake and open my eyes

The emptiness engulfs me from inside out

internally I scream manically yet on the outside silence enchains me

GOD, I really wish I was dreaming

Family affairs

divided family

in a divided time

they all put their love on the line

Father sleeps around again, with a woman from a bar

mother drinks too much wine

and gets into her car

father is beaten, for that woman was another mans wife

too much wine and behind the wheel

mother looses her life

lets not forget

the little boy

who is left on his own

no more family

eight years old living in a catholic children's home

a divided family

in divided graves

and that little boy

still feels the constant pain

My gook is gobbled

is there a purpose to a porpoise said the turtle to the tortoise

I dont know said the cat to the swan, i thought i knew but now its gone

They sat as the 4 friends wandered and pondered

on a journey in a land called wonder

(note) I have no idea on gods earth what I was on when I wrote this

Telletubbies

over the hills

and far away

Teletubbies come out to play

I take out my gun

take aim and shoot

bye bye Tinkywinky, Dipsy, lala and Po

Tellytubbies say oh no

(note) Most Likely written whilst on a hard comedown and they are creepy.

Headlines

here is the news at ten

woman raped by two unknown men

asian male murdered in frenzied racial attack

another celeb dies addicted to smack

police raid a notorious drug den

nothing new on the news at ten

(Note) Feeling Philosophical on an LSD comedown I believe

Memory Block

will you pass me that thing

what thing, that thing

that watsit that doodah ya know

what thing

that thing, with buttons and numbers on

oh you mean the phone

no

That watsit, that doodah, that thing

that changes the watsits on the thing

what thing

that thing you watch the ting on

you mean the remote

yes

will you pass me the remote

NO

(note) Not much to say about this one, It's just a silly little poem I wrote whilst highly stoned on Canabis and trying to ask my flatmate to pass me something.

hikoo number 1

facebooking my life

whilst having a nervous breakdown

was not a good idea

(note) Always sound advice, advise alas I failed to take on several occasions. Facebook and other social media became my soapbox, my way to vent and it cause so many problems on many an occasion.

Dragon

As I kiss the tender lips of the dragon

she takes my breath away and leaves me wanting more

oh so much more

Oh for the heat of her fierce fiery breath

That warms the coldness from deep within my slowly breaking fragile heart

haiku number 2

I sit and ponder

people wander softly, slowly by

what is on her mind

(note) In the early day of my recent sobriety I would walk into the city centre and sit and people watch. I would perch myself with my notebook and pen and just watch people rush by, caught up in their own little world.

Fallen Heroes

Love lorn soldiers in a war torn land

why must you die in the forgotten trenches of your countries hand

Fallen heroes

who will remember you

when the war is over an no longer in the news

Fallen heroes

in my memory you will survive

yet never again will you see your homes, children or wives

Fallen heroes

laid dying in the trenches alone

lay down your guns now and follow the angels

HOME

It's fate

It's fatality

It's the angel of the dead

It's anger

It's attitude

Its colour is red

The colour of blood

No sign of peace

and the number of casualties is absolute obese

(Note) Dedicated to the memory of my first real mentor and friend Captain Stephen Wormald. The Queens finest, the 2nd Battalion the Royal Anglian Regiment "The Poachers"! Sadly died when his Land Rover went over a mine, Bosnia 28th April 1994, Aged 28.

Sons of Normanton

There were only really two people from Normanton that ever really made anything of their lives, at least that I knew of. The first was the actor Reece Dinsdale, he did rather well appearing in a popular Television series in the 80s "Home to Roost" with John Thaw. I never really knew Reese that well to be honest. I knew his Parents Alan and Sally during my time at All Saint Church, my first try at Christianity. They were a lovely aging couple. One of my great lies as a younger man was the Reese was my Brother, when in fact all he ever was was the son of my sponsors at church. I had the pleasure of meeting him on a couple of occasions, I was always star struck. It has been my dream to work with him one day. Perhaps in the current circumstances it might actually be possible.

The Second was Captain Stephen Wormald, an Army Man. His Father attempted to teach me at Freeston High and his Mother attempted to reign me in at Went vale. I did meet Stephen quite a few times, he was such an inspiration. The first time I met him was in my week at Freeston. He was such an amazing man, an inspiration to man, to me.

I was such an emotional child with a hot temper. He found me over turning tables in a rage. He told me that I should call him a brother because brothers help each other, brothers are family, and brother tell brothers the truth, with respect and honour. Brothers also listen because sometimes brothers know best, especially the older ones. He told me anger was fine but we need to channel it into something honorable, like our country, our career or our art.

Stephen was killed when his armored vehicle hit a landmine in Bosnia in 1994.

His funeral was the biggest I have ever seen. The service was held at the church at Hightown. You couldn't move inside for the family and well wishers. The audio from the service was played through speakers on the outside so the hundreds of mourners could hear.

After the service he was taken to the graveyard a few hundred yards down the road. We marched mournfully in a line to pay our respects to the lost son of Normanton.

The bugle played the last post and people left, I stayed, I cried as I overlooked his coffin covered in roses. I gave a salute, for that's what brothers do, to say goodbye.

Illustration: M.J Hiblen 2017 – (c) Jack W Gregory

VIII

Human Zoo

We all suffer from fear. Fear of rejection, fear of failure, fear of the unknown, fear of our past, fear of fear. Fear is not limited, it is not discriminatory and neither is it unbound, it affects even the strongest of men, the strongest of minds.

Prison is the Place I fear.

There are so many subjects I could write about yet it always boils down to one thing that has haunted me, that has disturbed me but driven me for many years now.

Not that I have a wish to change my past or wish to forget or even regret my it, however none of these things can ever make up for the actions I took, the people I hurt, the way I lived and the choices I made. What I can do is learn from my actions, use my mistakes to educate other. I can use my past as a blueprint of how not to live and not to keep on making those same old mistakes again and again.

I have spent so many years living in the grips regret, letting guilt and shame haunt me to the point of breaking. What good did it ever do ?, the only thing these ways ever did was hurt me, and in the process caused damage to the ones I loved and those who loved me back.

My addiction to violence, to hate, to self harm (because addiction is a form of self harm)no longer rules over my life, not because I have forgotten them, or I ignore them, or even because they no longer bother me, because from time to time they do, it is simply because I am no longer a slave to fear, I am free in the knowledge that I am loved by so many who choose to let me be a part of their lives and it took me all too many years to realize it.

In writing this introduction to my prison based poems and thinking of its subject I needed a title, It could easily be called Things my family never knew I did or The Ballard of Shame (both of these were actual contenders for the title by the way).

The Prison reform system needs review, it is broken in so many ways. Being sent to prison is meant to be a punishment, so why do so many people seem to be institutionalized ?, why do so many re offend ?.

I believe it is this; Prison may keep the physical presence locked away, however a mind, a will, good or bad, habit and a behavior is much more difficult to mute. Prison conditions us, it gives us a routine, It can and has helped some such as myself to rehabilitate, however in my experience a cell can be just a box for comfort, it is when we build our own mental prisons and the danger begins.

The Prison system, the whole subject of Incarceration and to some extent the process that we go through upon imprisonment is greatly misunderstood on the outside.

Many people on the outside either misunderstand, some are plainly ignorant or simply uneducated about the whole subject of prisons and prison life, either that or they simply do not care. It seems to me that once we are criminalized we are to a point dehumanized and often Animalized. Once in prison we cease to have a name, we are a number,to an extent we become a commodity.

Recently The Eastern Daily Press recently published an article about prison meal, the keyboard warriors went ballistic, as If to say how dare the government let these animals eat this well, how dare they contemplate giving a healthy balanced meal to a convict. It's sad to read, difficult even. On one hand yes they are being punished for crime, yet it is my experience that many re offenders are stuck in the same loop, once release they are put back into the same situation that contributed to putting them there. There is little to no help of intervention, how can we expect offenders not to re offend when we do very little to get to the core of the problem.

Life is a journey that everyone has to take, we travel many a road to get where we are going. For some it is a straight path, for others it is a series of wrong turns and getting lost. Some like myself are lucky to find our way again, others are lost and unfortunately never find their way home.

As I have said, Prison was a difficult time in my life, a time that still haunts me, that still gives me nightmares and flashbacks. Prison did not rehabilitate me as such, but what it did do was give me the constant yearning and longing never to go back.

Since I have left the institution I have set foot in HMP Leeds once to visit my brother. I found it so difficult, even to write to him but that is how much that time affected me.

However now being a born again christian and wanting to carry the message of hope to the broken , my work with the church is leading me to work within the system to help in prisoner rehabilitation.

The poems in the following chapter are about my time within the HMP System …

The Fall

Scared so scared, what have I done?

has my life really accumulated to this living nightmare?

The years of pent up frustration, of hate and fear have now personified into an uncontrollable and violent rage.

Screaming, I was screaming

So loud, so hard my voice began to break

I could not, I would not stop

still I beat at his already broken face, his body now limp, almost lifeless as tears fall fiercely down my blooded bony and dirt stained cheeks.

The sourness and bitterness have poisoned my soul and here I am scared

So scared and alone

yet I don't even know if he still breathes.

The Nothingness could not come soon enough

not with a bang but with a crack and a thud as the light fades to dark with hints of Blue Lights and shouting

So much shouting, Inaudible yet apparent

Asleep, now asleep

Well I guess I am as only darkness now surrounds me

Silent

So Silent

As I sit in quiet contemplation

Considering the circumstances in which I find myself yet again

Wondering, Worrying If the actions I have taken over these past few days would have ended any differently had I not been a Madman In a chemically induced haze

Falling, I'm falling

Fast and hard, and that rock bottom I have been heading for my whole life is coming faster and harder than I ever thought possible

Devastation is Inevitable, The concept of freedom now implausible

I had walked into this establishment this morning of my own free will and still a free man

For now at least

Silent

So Silent

deafened by my own morbid and manic thoughts as they wildly bounce around my broken brain at a million miles an hour and they will not stop

Uncertain that they ever will

you see In my mind I am already imprisoned

and have been for a long time

but still physically free

I do not notice the time go by

or the other people aimlessly wondering from courtroom to courtroom

I don't even care if they go home or are locked up like I am certain to be, the only thing at the forefront of my mind is self preservation

I could still walk out of the front door a free man for now

until they catch me on the run

at least I would be free

For a while

at least

and I get up to leave and walk out the door

The Realization

Awake, I am awake

Barely

Awake from a violent nightmare, my head pounding and the pain begins.

Had I been to sleep ?, I did not remember going to bed, but hey, that was nothing new. Bright lights and blurriness attacked my already altered vision. Figures just out of sight waiting patiently, watching my every move

Confused and frightened, What had I done?

vastly unaware of events to come, I didn't even know where I now lay.

White walls and the all too familiar fragrance of vomit and disinfectant overtake my senses as it became apparent that a hospital room is where I now reside

Metal scraped metal as I moved my arm, apparent now I had become a prisoner in my bed

And the policeman nodded as if to say "Yeah mate, you know it, You're screwed"

I begin to scream in an uncontrollable rage

Hostility and anger ebbed from every single sweat filled pore, knowing in a moment the darkness will come again in the form of a liquid cosh

The darkness may be coming, yet sleep will elude me as it always does.

Fighting, thrashing to the very end as the cold sharp needle pierces my Arse cheek and the light begins to fade.

Sleep now comes, but at what price

XIV

Lady Justice

Is Lady Justice really blind or does she just cover her eyes so she cannot see the consequences of our actions ?, Does she weep when men like me find themselves on the wrong side of the bench ?

Had I been a better man

Had I been sorry for what I had done

I would have regret instead of this constant fear

Had I taken responsibility for my actions, My crimes then I would have apologized when given the opportunity instead of calling the magistrates all the names under the sun

and moon

and every known planet as a matter of fact

Utter contempt, utter disdain for these people who want nothing more than to lock me away

Take away my freedom and keep me in a Human Zoo

The swear words, the insults now firing rapidly

Would the sentence be lighter had I not been so frightened and hidden my fear behind a mask of anger? Had I not delivered that Final Fuck You ?

I Guess I will never know

Human Zoo

behind these walls of bricks, wire and mortar

men are caged

for some life here is absolute mental torture

door slams shut

they go into meltdown

enraged at the hand that life has dealt them

"Oh woe is me" they would say "I can't handle this for one more day"

Its put up or shut up

Beat-down or lock-down

a few solitary nights in the Hole

and your only company

your ever fading, darkened soul

Home

Prison is a home for the Broken

Annualized, Criminalized

A Thousand stares from the cold dead eyes of men Institutionalized

Untitled

No truer word

ever spoken

Prison is a Home for the broken

Lag

His once Green eyes now graying

as he wears the years upon his wrinkled face

a sadness now sits where his crooked smile used to sit

His body now draped, stooped

as a life lived here sits heavily upon his shoulders

his pride

now replaced by routine

weighing him down

deeper and deeper into the system

Institutionalized

17 when he arrived

now 55 and the years have been so unkind

so old for a man relatively so young

One mistake as a teenager put him there

a temper he could not keep, nor hide

yet in here is somehow an easier life

a daily routine

Slop out, work, eat and sleep

more friends on the inside than out

because on the outside looking in he found nothing but pain

so he fought and fought

just so he could live as a man

on the inside … institutionalized

Illustration by Bobby Harrison 2017 (used with permission)

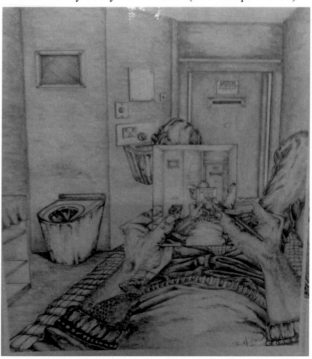

Life by numbers

Imagine this

if you can

if you will

a great length of time spent in a cell

six feet by eight

four walls and

a bed

no company for you

just the thoughts in your head

Twenty-Three hours a day

three six fie days a year

boxed in a room with resentment and fear

no longer a name

just a number for you

contemplating your actions

locked in that room

a mattress so thin

a sheet heavy and coarse

back hurts so much

skin blistered and sore

in the corner

a bucket sits

with no other contents but you urine and shit

twenty-three hours in that day

locked in that cell

tormented internally

struggling to keep the rage inside

nowhere to run

nowhere to hide

There is no glory for serving time

No medal, No trophy

for walking the line

only guilt and shame

like a chain around your neck

all you can know

is pain, hurt and regret

(Note) Written about solitary confinement

12 x 10 barred blues

Can't bloody sleep again

all that racket outside

as the boots of the Black and Whites bang on the steel walkway

It mess with my mind

My Pad mate is snoring again

he's making a din

so I make a shady rollie

from the dimps in my tin

I've run out of papers

to roll the baccy in

so I rip a page from my bible

its the book of Matthew I'm smoking

Still can't sleep

I might just kick off

at least if I do I'll get liquid kosh

I still won't sleep

I just won't care anymore

I'll just be care free and Dribblin on the old concrete floor

Road

Two Long Years of living in constant hate

That poisonous environment now behind me as I stand at the prison gates

Clear Polythene bag of possessions in hand

held over my shoulder, tied with an old rubber band

I've waited for this day for so long

yet sadness sits upon my chest

as everything I know and am used to now stands behind me

And

All I see is the same thing I saw from my window on those long and lonely days

The only thing before me is road

The Lad on B Wing

released at the same time

wears a smile as his family greet and cheer

yet for me there is no one here

Perhaps the bus driver will give me a smile or a nod

in recognition of where I have been

where I was

They say home is where your heart is

so what about the friends I have just left whose hearts belong to the broken
system

Institutionalized

I will not, I can not look back

In fear tears may fall as I walk that asphalt path into unfamiliar territory

and the road will take me wherever she leads

<u>XV</u>

Paul Sykes

Paul Sykes was a Champion Heavyweight Boxing Champion from Lupset in Wakefield.

I can't really say that Paul Sykes a friend, he was an acquaintance at best. I first met Paul in the mid 90's whilst I was working a job Leeds way. The Job required muscle and a certain way that none of us were accustomed to, Paul was recommended. Paul ran a debt collecting racket called The Last Resort Debt Collection agency. I work with Paul and for Paul several times, I won't actually say what was done or what happened but what I will say is it put me off of debt collecting for life.

I didn't think about Paul for many years until I started speaking to author Jamie Boyle about his Book Sykes: Unfinished Agony. After seeing one of my poems on Facebook asked me if I would write some for his book, which I did. He didn't use all the poems so I thought I would share them In My book. I will start with the ones from unfinished agony.

Enjoy !!!

The Last Resort Debt Collection Agency

Whatever is your pleasure

whether it's for a tipple, smack, cars or coke

I don't care

Whatever your situation

If you don't pay I will be there

Knocking at your door

If you owe you pay

full stop

I don't care about your needs

or whether it's fifty or a thousand quid

if you don't

I'll take it out of your hands, face and knees

If you're not home

when I come knocking

beware

maybe your mum will answer when I knock

I'll make her a pop of tea

tell her what you owe the money for

and what a naughty boy you have been

and if she cannot pay your debt, I'll take her scooter and TV

If I have to come back again

the debt will double bubble

and when I do find you

mind your manners

cos old Syksey's coming

I'll blacken both your eyes

I'll break yer bleadin nose

I'll take my time to punish you

I'll even break your toes

you won't ever see coming

I'll hit you hard and fast

if you don't have the cash

your face is getting smashed

so if you can't pay what you owe

if you have taken out a loan

and if you knew when you took it, you could not pay what you owe

Then son you will regret it

you had better run, you had better hide

Syksey is coming to get it

UNFINISHED AGONY

His fists, those fists
Forged by iron and fire

The fire, that fire
That burned deep into his soul

The Contender

Yet beneath the furnace that
Fueled him, a heart of stone
Had begun to for and the fire
Suffocated quickly

The life force that drove him
Began to fade

His agony was born

From the glamorous life, the
Prize winning ring to obscurity
Behind bars

The agony that filled him
Became sweet as it fermented
Into a symbioses of pure hate
And pish

Unabridged agony

His mind once so quick and full
Of knowledge became the cave
Of a savage mad man

The eyes, those eyes
That once shone brighter than

most now vacant
The windows to his soul now a
Mirror to his madness

Those fists his fists became
The last resort

God help those who get in his
Way

Violence personified became
Him

His unadulterated agony, only as
Strong as his libido

Yet the agony unfurled as his
Only sustenance came in a can

Contender to criminal
Criminal to joke
As his last days are spent
Aimlessly wandering in a
Chemically induced haze

From contender to grave
Leaving an Unfinished Agony

Facing John L

There he stands
Fallen from grace
Bruises on his hands
Blood drips from his face

His heart heavy as
Disappointment sets in
for this was the fight
he could not win

He did not train
He drank instead
Went into the fight in which his
Heart ruled his head

As the bell rang for the final time
The Contender knew his career
Was on the line

As punches connected to his
Head, to his face
He knew this fight would end in
Disgrace

The bell rang again and the fight
Had finished, The Contender
Knew his career was diminished

THE AGONY OF SYKES

Alone Alone
The Hobo is as the Hobo was
Alone Alone
To the very end

Ignored as they pass him by
Alone Alone
In his helpless life

Who he is now is not who he Was
Along the way he had become
Lost and now he is alone alone

A contender a great in the
Boxing world destined for
Legendary status

Yet he sits alone alone
The streets of Wakefield now his
Home

His friend in a can offers
Comfort and peace, yet he is
Alone alone
Left to die on the streets

Ignored by his peers
A joke to some he once called friends
Yet he sits in the doorway
With his Special friend
Alone alone
Till the very end

Westgate bound

There is a name Etched on the minds of many

Synonymous with trouble

The epitome of madness incarnate.

The lost son of lupset Out on the blitz Looking for a fight yet again and it's barley turned Tuesday.

He Loved by some Hated by many

It's Paul 'bleedin' Sykes

The Townly chucked him out again

watch out he is city bound

Wandering aimlessly Westgate way, much to the dismay of black tied bouncers that would no doubt stand toe to toe by the end of the night.

Face to face

Trouble and larger stain his breath

Passers by wear a smile like a mask to hide the fear that the mad man may snap

His jagged lips grin from behind his bearded face, no shirt no shoes only dirty joggers and a football top

"Come on pal let me in"

Much to his disdain, the answer is NO and now a grimace replaces his crooked smile

Nothing now but anger and hate

Violence imminent

The trouble now starts fists are thrown police are called

a taxi ride in a Black Mariah now imminent

content in the context of discontent for tomorrow is another night to fight

It's Paul 'Bleedin' Sykes

Roadman

Standing at the gates of the prison he called home

The former mountain man of Wakefield stands alone

A mere shadow of his former self

And his life is fading and fading

Not looking forward for the fear of looking back

Eyes to the gray asphalt covered ground Unsteady, uneasy He is Wakefield bound

Back to the streets , Back to the pain

Back to the place they all know his name

Syksey the tramp

Only got himself to blame

At least that's what they say

Only deserves to sleep in a dilapidated doorway

Doesn't he?

His old friend Stella, She won't disappoint

Her warm kiss will comfort him

at least keep him in a slumped sedated state So he could remain blissfully ignorant of the forthcoming hate

Once a boxer of champion breed

Who traveled the county and sewed his seed

A life of fame stood before him

A bestselling book

Yet like so many men before him

The drink messed him up

Toe to Toe

There Paul was
Toe to toe
Trapped in a dance of reciprocity with a man half his height But twice as
wide
yet neither would back down

eyes locked in a constant stare
the air thick and heavy with the inaudible grunts and growls
of the booze filled trolls
loitering about
Jabbering, jeering
Stirring the proverbial melting pot

"Crack him Paul" a little runt shouts
"go on Paul, knock the bleeder out"
vomit on the floor
the brown bile soaks into his nice white trainers
Turning them a light shade of shite
Now big Paul is anchoring for a fight

However the other bloke aint small
Looks like he could throw a few
But by the look on his face he is gonna puke
And poor Ol Sykesy doesn't know what to do
Cos one good crack and its not just his trainers covered in spew

Story of Paul

Here are stories of a man named Sykes

Tales of violence, prison, Trouble and strife

From those who knew him

And his troubled life

From experience Let me tell you this

Although his moods were hit and miss

His fists they never were

To look in to his aging eyes

To see the pain personified

To see the anger build inside

And feel his gaze intensified Burn you to your soul

You know that he might blow

To know a man so volatile

And verbally so versatile

So many secrets behind that smile

His words could beat you down

A contender once

The world was at his feet

Yet It wasn't a man that had him beat

It was Stella who brought him to his knees

And took him to the streets

The man that once would break your bones Died on those streets

Broken and alone

Illustration M.J Hiblen 2017 – (c) Jack W Gregory

The Agony of Me:My Mental Illness and I

XVI

The Black Dog Barks

For so many years, more than I care to think of I have battled against the Black Dog of Mental Illness. So many Times I has fought and almost lost. So many self destructive events, countless suicide attempts and overdoses. My Mental Illness has often walked side by side with my addiction, although the two are not exclusive.

For so many years my creativeness has been somewhat of a bane to me, yet causes me so much joy, It has been somewhat of an oxymoron.

Mental Illness is still misunderstood, It still carries a stigma and the amount of times I have been told to man up is ridiculous. My writing has been my biggest crutch although has caused me the most pain; Pain of the broken promises, the rejection, the times I have been told I will never make it, I will never finish anything, you are not good enough, well it has left me heartbroken so many times and with heartbreak comes darkness, at least for me anyway.

Here are a small collection of poems that have been written in many a different state, at varying times through trials, through breakdowns and Let downs.

These words are from a man at the different stages of Brokenness.

A lack of luster

Silent

It's never silent

at least not in my head

for the black dog is ever barking

Silence would be a blessing, silence would be a gift

It has never been just silent

from the thoughts that race a thousand miles per hour to the screaming that never seems to stop

The next big idea, a poem or two or three or four

or Perhaps a dozen or so

maybe more

I am constantly losing count

Unfinished stories, songs and symphonies with no end

Constant, incessant thoughts of suicide beat louder than any drum at the back of my mind

I would have killed myself years ago were it not for the yearning to actually complete something before I slip the mortal coil, or maybe I was just too unorganized, too lazy to actually finish the job.

God knows I have tried, a dozen or more times

yet even then those attempts were half hearted, half arsed and half finished. feeling so useless I could not even kill myself correctly.

Scared of life, scared of death and fighing for moments of sanity between the madness

Fearful so fearful

of the unknown, of the known and the bits in between, scared of nothing but scared of everything at the same time an Oxymoranic moron full of Lackluster and mental illness

Yet through it all one thing and one thing only kept those things at bay, only one thing would even calm the storm

even then there would never be silence, there would never be peace, only one thing would calm my mind to a slower pace and put me and my black dog to sleep

This Life

This Life, My life

is a constant fight to stumble through the darkness

because I am

Petrified, terrorized by the blinding light

Unspoken

silently I sit

words rest upon my lips

unspoken

yet not unsaid

as they mimic my brokenness

through my aging graying eyes

Dreamer

You're living in a dream mate

Take your head out of the clouds

Come back to reality

Put your feet firmly back on the ground

You've gotta grow up and belt up

your chasing an impossible, implausible dream

We love you mate, but at times you make us want to scream and shout, slap you about, knock you out of your constant Daydream

You will NEVER be a writer mate just face it

A dream is a dream don't chase it

Its money that puts food on the table not poetry

Not Un-obtainable, Un-realistic goals

If you carry on the way you do mate, you will always be on the dole

We don't say this to hurt you

we love you

honestly we do

But if you carry on like this mate

You are well and truly SCREWED!!!

(note)I have lost count on the amount of times I have been told I will fail at being a writer, I suppose that is the main reason I have held myself back and have not written anything for publication before this, except my contributions to Jamie Boyle's Sykes Books.

Tears

As the tears fall

from the windows to my soul and trickle down my aging face

they rest upon my lips and bitterness now sits

where the words once rested

i am so confused and devastated by the complexity on my own fear

of my own fears

A constant state of confusion

here I sit

in

quiet contemplation

at war with myself

on one hand remembering the destruction

yet knowing without destruction my life would be over

but still, my will

is

split indefinitely

I fight   I think   I fall

my ego is a complete

oxymoron

(note) The Black Dog was well and truly barking in my face when I wrote this. The noise was at times deafening. I could not silence the constant stream of a thousand thoughts a minute. I sit on the floor of my Bedsit cradling my head, Sobriety was only an infant instilled in me on this instance. I just wanted to scream at the top of my voice, however I feared the echoes of my madness would go unheard as it always did, so I suffered silently as I cried myself to sleep.

Memories

Memories from my shaded past

darken the route of my life's path

With hardened heart and fists clenched tight

I learned to fight my way through life

Drunken punch ups, scraps and scrapes

and that was just between me and my mates

Getting wrecked, committing crime

is how I spent the vast amount of my time

I do not regret the way I lived

but I am sorry for the things I did

The friends and family and dignity lost

well that was the most expensive and extensive cost

I cannot change the past, nor do I wish to block it out

I have more than a few skeletons in my closet, it's more like a Graveyard

without a shadow of a doubt

I'm not the man I used to be

I'm different in every way

From the wreck I once was

To the man I am today

Betwixt

betwixt the midst of personal sleepless slumber

in the ether of madness succumbed

stand I

fallen from grace

and in the midst of the mouth of madness

sanity comes in waves

I am a broken man

my mind in absolute tatters

and yet a gentle tug at my hearts strings

may cause my life to shatter

if I sleep now, I may never awaken

this is more than sanity failing, a depressive and deadly state

emotionally i am blinded by my own fear and loathing

spiritually dead, numbness engulfs my fragile state

screaming so loud I am deafened by my own silence

no one can hear me

I silently suffocate inside my own maddening state

Clock

Tick Tock

The hands on the clock

ticking life away

second by second

minute by minute

hour by hour

day by day

Then we look back to yesterday and say

how many more seconds

how many more minutes

how many more hours

how many more days

the inevitability, life always has to end

More tears

As the tears fall

from the windows to my soul and trickle down my aging face

they rest upon my lips and bitterness now sits

where the words once rested

i am so confused and devastated by the complexity on my own fear

of my own fears

Unspoken

silently I sit

words rest upon my lips

unspoken

yet not unsaid

as they mimic my brokenness

through my aging graying eyes

Cry

Tears they fall

from my aging eyes

and they dry upon the life stained mirrors to my soul

Broken

Broken

Fr-ag-me-nt-ed

internally tormented

to the point of madness incarnate

Numb

mind awry

with a million thoughts

raging, silently raging

numb, so numb

as the madness comes

in the form

of loneliness incarnate

Mirror cracked

broken

but never beaten

walking tall

standing firm

my body may bruise and break

my strength from the inside shall never be defeated

only stunned

yet the mirror cracks

Silent

It's never silent

at least not in my head

for the black dog is ever barking

Silence would be a blessing, silence would be a gift

It has never been just silent

from the thoughts that race a thousand miles per hour to the screaming that never seems to stop

The next big idea, a poem or two or three or four

or Perhaps a dozen or so

maybe more

I am constantly losing count

Unfinished stories, songs and symphonies with no end

Even More Tears

Tears form

Born of fear and grief

soul bereft

all that is left is a tear stained handkerchief

Illustration: M.J Hiblen 2017 – (c) Jack W Gregory

Playground battleground

The sun shining

Burning Brightly on this gentle July Afternoon

heat kisses the back of my neck, yet the slow, soft Summer breeze cools the skin on my aging face and it feels nice

So nice !

so there I sit silently

my gaze fixed upon her beauty

and she dances to the playful tune of childhood

skipping and laughing

she, away on her travels, her imagination working overtime

having an adventure in her own personal wonderland

so I wear a look of pride and love upon my face

a look every doting father will wear

playground now full

other children joyfully playing to their own childhood songs as their
parents look upon them with a similar gaze to my own

so I smile

yet as she plays, she plays alone and sadness begins to haze my View

yet she smiles

and I wonder why

her playful spirit now interrupted and she is taken away from her
wonderland in one fleeting moment as she rushes to the aid of an injured
child

to her, in her mind he is an injured comrade fallen in the battle of the
playground war

wounded

his knees grazed, he shaking, crying filled with fear

and She ever caring

her instinct overtakes and she looks upon her fallen friend with the same
loving stare I seen so many times before

the same loving look she gave her father all too many times before

It's empathy personified

her words wise

reassuring, calming

and healing comes as it always does as she smiles

his crying now a gentle sob as his fear begins to subside

she is so old

for one so young !

as she gazes lovingly at his tear stained and dirty face

her smile turns to grin as she softly says

Wanna Play ?

she takes him by the hand

friends now for the lifetime of her stay in the playground battleground

knowing in reality she may never see him again when daddy takes her home

yet she smiles

And I still wonder why

So, there I sit silently, peacefully for the first time in a long time

filled with pride

and once again

I feel nice

its so nice to feel nice

XVIII

Ballard of a broken man

So there I was on the tail end a particularly bad nervous breakdown, still somewhat a broken man. My life being full of deliberate excesses of anything I could get my hands on had accumulated in nearly losing everything I held dear. I had been living in the spare room of a much younger friend, before that I had been homeless. I know deep down that I cannot blame anyone else for the way my life had turned out, although I would have blamed the milkman for my shortcomings if I could have.

A couple of weeks before my life was a spiral of confusion and pain. My self indulgence, my own jaded mind and a heart for nothing more than selfishness caused mayhem for many around me, Including my daughter who would have been around 7 at the time. I could not have blamed her if she had said she never wanted to see me again, I am thankful she is a strong little girl with a love for her daddy that would not fade.

By that time I was in a strong enough mental state to have her at the weekends again. Every Saturday morning we would walk it the couple of miles walk into the city from where I was living. On the way there is a beautiful little park surrounded by beechnut and horse chestnut trees.

Knowing my head all I wanted to do was get to the city so I could sit down and have a nice fat latte, however I caved on to those deep blue hypnotic eyes and took he into the park to watch her play.

I had started writing again a week or so before and carried a blue and pen, so I said yes and wrote this sitting on the park bench whilst I watched her play.

XIX

Redemption through salvation

For so many years I experimented with Religion. I Tried Everything from Christianity to Islam, Buddhism to Wicca and never quite found what I was looking for. I was constantly searching for ways to be a better person, to not be addicted or mentally ill anymore, yet all seemed lackluster.

Christianity is always the one that I returned to yet when everything eventually and inevitably turned sour and I could not get what I wanted, what I thought I needed then I would blame the people, blame the church and blame God, yet I never looked at my own failings, my own shortcoming . I guess its easier to blame God than take full irreconcilability for my own self destructive behavior.

It is only when I was in hospital and I thought I had lost everything, that my world had collapsed did I accept Jesus into my life. The people from a church that barely knew me came to visit every single day, tried to feed me, to mop my brow and to love me despite the verbal abuse I gave them. They would not stop loving me, they would not give up on me and saw me through an extremely difficult time in my life. I love my church family at Hope Community Church Wymondham very much.

Dream

I dreamed I met my lord last night

and I listened whilst he talked

he reminded me of the difficult path through life that I have walked

we laughed and cried together

as the memories tumbled by

and just as heartache turned to anger

I asked the question why

why did you not protect me

when my body was abused

why could you not have stopped me

when i picked up, drank and used

that was your path in life he said

the way it had to be

it made you strong and brave and wise

and led you back to me

my precious child I love you

I never left your side

I was your heartbeat and breath

the times you nearly died

I dreamed I met my lord last night

and he listened whilst I spoke

I told him of my gratitude that my spirit had awoke

Debt

I had a debt

a debt I could not pay

yet the slate was wiped clean so I could live my life today

a debt so big that money could not clear

only the pain of a man that died without fear

and since man is broken

the only way it could be done

was for a loving father

to send himself as his son

so there he was

for a debt that was ours

on a hill in Golgotha

nailed to a tree

he took all of the sin and slowly suffocated for you and me

and

as the blood fell from his hands, feet and head

he yelled 3 words

"it is finished"

and then he was dead

by his death

he put in a guaranteed cheque

the wages of sin

paid by his death

so how do we access life where we are no longer in debt with sin

simply by just

believing in him

(note) The one thing I always struggled with about Christianity is the concept of Grace. I mean really, How could God love a man like me ?.

So we are Almost at the end of the apocalypse or if you prefer to call it, the end of this slightly depressing book.

I can only call them Miscellaneous or bits and bobs

These are the rest of the Poems that don't really fit into a category or chapter. Poems I have written In various frames of mind.

Enjoy!!!

Daddy

he will catch you

when you fall

he will love you

most of all

he would fight

and he would die

just to stand at

his daughters side

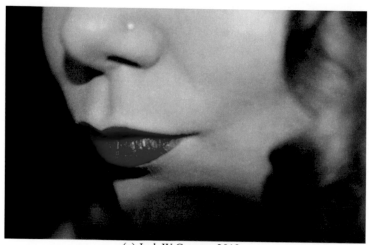

Beauty

beauty sits

upon the lips

of the one

who beholds her

Woman

She is woman

beautiful, strong

in quiet contemplation

every word that sits upon her beautiful lips

becomes a weapon

her every thought ammunition

She will love you

until she becomes broken

or until it kills

on the inside

it is not by hate

it is by love she is driven

Mum

she would walk

a thousand miles

just to make you smile

to wipe away the salty tears

to fight away your pain and fears

just because she loves you

Father

his love

unabridged, unbound

two hearts

now beat as one

unconditionally

a fathers love

Eternal

Pray for London

Words they escape me

confuse, anger and dismay me

I cannot see the sense in this

this isn't something to dismiss

we can never forget the events of that day

the injured, the dead, the senseless violence

the world now at silence

for the actions of one man taking extreme to a whole new measure

and we are left bewildered

Devastated

For nothing now will ever be the same again

London has fallen

and all we can do is silently weep

for all those who were injured and died

on that Westminster street

(note) On 22 March 2017,Khalid Masood carried out a terrorist attack that took place near of the Palace of Westminster in London, seat of the British Parliament. He drove his car into tourists and passers by. He injured more than 50 people and killed 4. After he crashed the car he knifed and killed an unarmed Police officer, he was shot dead at the scene by an armed Police officer. This poem was written on hearing of those events.

Shhhhhh (a silly little interlude)

Cough cough

splutter splutter

sniff sniff

mutter mutter

shhhhh the films about to start

i really think i have to.......

SNEEZE

and I dont have a handkerchief

haha

calm down, ill use my sleeve

or yours

OK OK, just kidding mate

really, please don't start

really

I gotta

....

Happy families

happy little family

on a happy little hill

a happy little boy

a happy little girl

Happy little families on happy little hills

yeah sure, get real

ADROPHOBIA

massive savings on windows and doors

cheapskate holidays, magical mystery tours

buy our limited edition crap

Dissatisfaction garenteed of none of your money back

low cost loans

clear your debts for a fee

for nothing in this life comes for free

Business man

business man

designer clothes

mobile phone

gold plated and bold

business man

make your business decisions

don't pay your taxes, go directly to prison

Man in the moon

as I look up into the night sky

there is one thing that catches my eye

I see the light from the moon shining down on me

Jack W Gregory 2016

Street life

It is cold

I am cold

so bloody cold

shaking, trembling

as the blue winds blow

blistering, tormenting

I am cold

so cold

Cold, Scared and Alone

so alone

The bitterness it bites me

whips at my fragile face

I am cold

so cold

Confused, hungry, exposed

the elements are killing me

I am so full of guilt and shame

I dare not show the fear upon my face

my aging, chapped face

in fear that I may be ridiculed

I may be homeless but I can not be seen to be weak

or vulnerable to anyone let alone those who smile when they see me her

for my own stupid fault, I hurt them

they deserve to laugh at me and I deserve nothing more that the pain I have dished out

personified tenfold

So I lay down

in this cold lonely doorway

no food, no money

no blanket for me

Do you know what its like

to live outside the light

shrouded in a blanket of darkness

as people blinkered pass you by

either unable or unwilling to see you as you sit cold

emaciated and starving for more than just food.

It is so cold

I am so cold

Hungry, angry, alone

The night is setting in so quickly

The colder it gets

Hungry, so hungry

My stomach aches so badly

growling, aching

Oh how I wish there was sustenance in broken pride

I would be fat and full

But there is no nutritional value in a sandwich made of nothing but regret

I could cry

I want to, so bad

but I can not

For those salt laden tears will not feed me

It is to cold to sleep

and I just want to fade into oblivion

and if God loves me he will leave my hypothermic and take me in my cold induced state

either that or a hospital bed for the night

or two

at least It is warmer than this

because it is cold

so cold

I feel it deep into my bones

So I will walk the night long

at least whist I walk I will not freeze

and the streets are waking now

waking to the beat of the night time

so I will walk

to wherever my feet may go

anything, everything

to keep away the cold

For me the issue of Homelessness is as painful as Prison for me, If not more. My experience of homeless may not be as harsh as some, I had the odd sofa to crash down on a few nights a week the last time I was homeless, but It is painful non the less. I take full responsibility for the situation I ended up in, my life was an absolute me, a joke and the life I lived, the lies I told all contributed to my downfall, I have no one to blame but myself. I wanted to finish on this poem, not to end on a darker or depressing note, but because it has taken me full circle. My Life is so much better now, I am in a better place Mentally, Physically and Spiritually. I sincerely Hope that you have enjoyed the book ...Jack

IN LOVING MEMORY OF

MARY MAGDELINE MARGARET BISSETT

(Mum)

07/06/59 – 09/07/17

AND

LUNA MARY BISSETT

(Niece)

09/07/17 – 14/07/17

Afterword by Lee Wortley & Kelly Valerie McLean

During our extensive research into material based on historical facts befitting to a series of books myself and my dear friend and business partner Kelly Valerie Mclean are currently in the process of writing. A name kept creeping in repeatedly from the four corners of the world of social networking, a name that seemed all-encompassing within the current realms of independent film-making, poetry and many other areas of creative writing.

Our union was soon to be realized while deliberating over a widely debated fight that never came to fruition, between two giants of the Unlicensed Ring. None other than that of Lenny 'The Guv'nor' Mclean and Paul Sykes!

Over the odd meet, the three of us sat around a table and exchanged ideas for a short film based on Mclean and Sykes. I the trainspotting researcher, Jack the budding film maker and of course Kelly the one and only Daughter of one of our chief protagonists. While getting to know one another, it soon became apparent to Kelly and I that our new-found friend Jack had been through the ringer on more than one occasion. Now, Jack has fought off many demons over the years as he strove to make a name for himself in the world of the Arts, from the dole-drums and back again choosing creativity as a defense mechanism, a literary battering ram if you will, with the sole aim of warding off his many debilitating mental and physical instabilities.

Among the many colorful pages of the ambiguous set of rhythmic words found in this book, Jack's disclosed piece entitled, (This is me) is indeed a favorite of ours, and, as Kelly and I have come to know Jack more and more, it is plain for us both to see that Jack chooses words as his addiction, his deity, in a last-ditch attempt of keeping at bay the dragon that once lurked outside his door. I and Kelly wish Jack every success with this insightful Book, the success that our friend Jack is wholeheartedly deserved of.

Jack Gregory ... by Jamie Boyle

Where do I start with Jack W. Gregory?

I came across Jack through writing my own book about the notorious Paul Sykes. Jack had had a couple of dealings with the caveman of Wakefield because those were the shady circles that Jack moved in then.

Jack is very open and honest about his past and the things that he got up to in his earlier years and will be the first to admit that he was once a drug addict and therefore lived the kind of lifestyle that comes with that. He was party to robberies, he dished beatings out and he scammed folk that were none the wiser of the fact that they were being scammed, he did bare knuckle boxing for money and anything else really to make a quick quid.

I'm delighted to say however that Jack changed his way of life and I mean seriously changed his ways. The first thing that struck me about him when we became friends was how intelligent he was, I don't think anyone expects ex drug addicts to be intelligent but he is intelligent in a way that it just seems to come naturally, he makes it look easy. The poems, the writing basically anything Jack W. Gregory turns his hand to he seems to do with great ease. Jack has a natural flair for words and in the short time I have known him I have turned to him myself for calming words of wisdom and I know pretty much that if I follow his advice I will not go far wrong. I know that may be hard to believe for the people that knew Jack 15 years ago and they might smile or even laugh that he is sought after for advice but that is the true measure of just how far he has come, it takes courage to change, a weak man will not see his faults and will stay the same throughout his life, making the same mistakes over and over.

Another major change in Jacks life which was instrumental in his personal change was that he found Jesus. Jack is deeply committed to following the Lord and I can only say that I am in awe of you Jack, my Brother. Long may you gain from the fruits of being clean, sober and from your love of the Lord Jesus Christ.

Philippians 4:13

'I can do all things through Christ who strengthened me'

That to me there, that one sentence sums up what Jack is about now, he can achieve anything he puts his mind to.

Now you're on your way up Jack, please don't look back, only ever forward, you don't have people in your life now who set you up for failure, you have good people who want you to succeed in everything you do.

The sky is the limit for you now, you put your trust in the Lord and had the courage to take control of your destiny. God Bless you and I look forward to watching your continued success.

Your friend,

Jamie Boyle x